Messaging for YOUR Business – Pocket Edition

TABLE OF CONTENTS

Contents

TABLE OF CONTENTS 1
Messaging from YOUR Business 2
    Welcome Message 2
    About YOUR Instructor/Author 3
Content Objectives 3
MESSAGING for YOUR New Business 4
    Overview of MESSAGING for Business 4
    Selecting YOUR Target Audience 5
    Having a Business Plan 8
    Deciding on YOUR Business Name 20
Other Resources 30

DISCLAIMER: This resource is NOT supported or endorsed by any individuals or businesses in the content. The text, links and samples are merely examples to illustrate the topic. The author/editor did not receive kickbacks, whether monetary or not, to mention anything in this book or the course online.

Additionally, this book makes no claim about the success you will have by following the steps or ensure you will make higher than usual profits because of following the processes – even if completed in order.

1 - @HnTDesignMedia

A Guide to Consistent Messaging for Business

Congratulations on taking steps towards YOUR business success!

Messaging from YOUR Business

Welcome Message

We are glad you are joining us!

Throughout these topics, you will learn about how to be consistent with the message you send out from your business to the marketplace. You will gain perspective on what is needed to tell the world exactly what you and your business stand for and what you represent.

We are going to discuss how to select your target audience, the importance of having a business plan and deciding on the name of your business that will stand the test of time.

This information will help YOU to know the level of work that must be put in throughout your journey. This will enable you to capture the most amount of market share with the highest level of profitability.

Messaging for YOUR Business – Pocket Edition

About YOUR Instructor/Author

My name is Beverly Reynolds!

I am a well-seasoned designer, corporate trainer and project manager with over 20 years of instructional experience. My work has been seen and viewed at large corporate entities and several top, world-wide Fortune companies.

In addition to the corporations at which I have been employed, I have started several businesses out of my home for remote and local clients.

Some of the work I have completed from home includes newspaper articles, feature magazine stories, animated course content, video scripting, flyer design, social media layout and more.

I look forward to sharing my experience and helping you too!

Content Objectives

We will cover details surrounding the following:

- *An overview of messaging*
- *Selecting YOUR target audience*
- *The importance of having a business plan*
- *Deciding on the name of YOUR business*

A Guide to Consistent Messaging for Business

MESSAGING for YOUR New Business

Overview of MESSAGING for Business

Many people think when they hear this word... that conveying a business proposition is easy.

They often assume that if they come up with a name and a slogan AND then tell their friends, that clients will flock to their door. There are so many more logistics to consider that we will soon discuss.

The main goal of the message that you send out is consistency. No matter what you say, you MUST say those words with confidence at regular intervals and on a consistent basis.

EXERCISE:

What kind of message does your business convey to the marketplace?

_____

_____

_____

_____

Messaging for YOUR Business – Pocket Edition

Selecting YOUR Target Audience

There are several factors to consider when selecting your audience.

Before we talk about the factors, we must define target audience. Your audience is the type of person or persona that is most likely to purchase or value your products or services.

Let's look at the main factors individually.

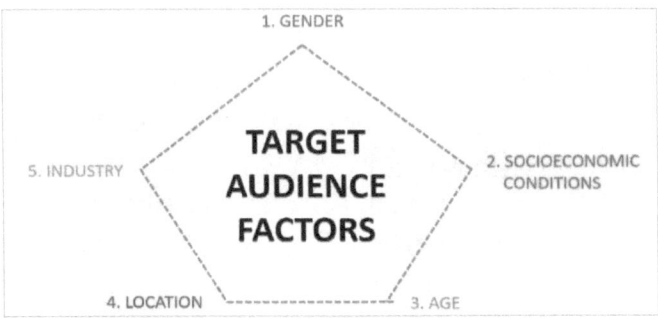

Figure 2: Factors that contribute to YOUR overall business audience

CHALLENGE: While you are targeting a specific audience, don't limit your marketing to that group so as to NOT limit your sales potential.

1. Your target audience for a make-up product is less likely to be a group of men versus women. Blush, mascara and other personal beauty products are also much more likely

A Guide to Consistent Messaging for Business

to be bought by females over males. Therefore, the wording, colors, fonts and overall look and feel should appeal to a specific group. When you create your materials, consider GENDER.

CHALLENGE: Think of ways to market your offerings based on gender. Determine how your marketing materials will differ – perhaps between items.

2. Alternatively, if you are marketing a high-dollar water cleansing system, then the SOCIOECONOMIC group you market to would be that of a higher-end audience which appreciates elegant design. Know how to structure your publications for different monetary or learning levels.

3. Now let's look at AGE. If your product or service is tailored to a younger crowd, it may be appropriate to have flashy colors and bold fonts, as well as an edgy design.

4. If you are targeting a marketing campaign in a specific state, it may be acceptable to use lingo from that region of the country. For

example, if I were to advertise an event to be held in Texas during the rodeo, it may be acceptable to state, "Hey, ya'll! Come to our tamale-eating contest at the fair!"

That sort of phrasing might not be as widely-accepted in a different part of the country. Therefore, GEOGRAPHY matters.

5. Finally, let's talk about INDUSTRY. Sometimes people look for ads placed in the industry for which they work. This may be because people tend to buy from who they know.

   When I visited New Orleans with my family while working in the death care industry, I sought out ads for the cemeteries that are unique to this area of the country. I was already familiar with the practices outside this city of rich, Southern history. Therefore, industry was key to my interests.

In conclusion, several of the most common factors to consider when planning your business include: GENDER, SOCIOECONOMIC CONDITIONS, AGE, LOCATION or GEOGRAPHY and INDUSTRY.

A Guide to Consistent Messaging for Business

EXERCISE:

What is the target audience for YOUR business?

_____

_____

Name ways you can use geography to your advantage in business?

_____

_____

Having a Business Plan

There are several aspects of a business plan.

All your planning must be documented in a book or electronically so your purpose is clear to yourself, those joining your business and your clients.

Your business plan is the basis of your business when questions arise and lays out a clear vision for the direction. Here are the areas that MUST be present in a business plan PRIOR TO naming your company or designing your logo.

Messaging for YOUR Business – Pocket Edition

	Tool	*Details*
Researching	Notepad / Paper	• Determine the demand for YOUR business
Summarizing (Building Blocks)	Spreadsheet tool	• Measurable, time-based goals • Fact-based objective • Create a mission statement
Employing (Staffing)	Indeed.com, HotJobs.com, LinkedIn.com	• Detailed ads to hire talented contractors, team members, employees • Roles and responsibilities to account for growth
Functioning	Spreadsheet tool	• Identify costs of doing business by location – both current and projected (including zoning laws, state or local taxes and tax breaks based on government programs, technology or job creation)

A Guide to Consistent Messaging for Business

	Tool	Details
Marketing	Adobe® PhotoShop™, Adobe® Illustrator™	• Known advertising costs • Design work
Budgeting	QuickBooks, Microsoft® Excel™, Spreadsheet tool	• Plan of how you will keep costs low • Budget statement

Figure 3: Image depicting the milestones of a business plan

We have already looked at several conditions, now let's look at the big picture and narrow down your scope so your business can begin to take shape. The ability to grow is based on careful planning and good decision-making skills – everyday.

Start by RESEARCHING the viability of your projected business offering and if there is a need for your services.

When you are SUMMARIZING your business, be sure to write down an overview of what you would like your ideal business to look like. Be sure to have a section for your goals and objectives.

Your goals should be measurable and based on a time frame. Your objective should by fact-based.

Messaging for YOUR Business – Pocket Edition

Don't forget to size up your competition. Determine what they are doing and what you can offer that solves a challenge in the market place.

Famous Person Quote about Goals
"If you want to live a happy life, tie it to a goal. Not to people or things."

-Albert Einstein

EXERCISE:

What are the three <u>main</u> goals of your business?

Daily:
_____

_____

Weekly:
_____

_____

Annually:
_____

_____

A Guide to Consistent Messaging for Business

How will you <u>measure</u> each of the above goals?

Daily:
_____
_____

Weekly:
_____
_____

Annually:
_____
_____

What is your fact-based business objective?
_____
_____

What challenge does your business solve?
_____
_____

Messaging for YOUR Business – Pocket Edition

Next, add details for <u>EMPLOYING</u>. Your business may have you being a solopreneur at first, but if you are going to scale your business in many markets, you will have to hire staff and manage all operations from the top-level. This could require ads on several job sites.

You will need to constantly be thinking of the roles and positions for each location as well as the detailed levels of responsibility and accountability.

Some of these people will know the proprietary details of your company, while other members of the team will not be included in this level of information. All members – regardless of level – deserve respect.

No matter the people hired into your organization, always be thinking about how each person can aid you in the growth of the business.

You will have to account for the time and resources of firing and letting go of team members that end up not being a good fit for your business – even after having been hired into your organization and you will need to replace these talents.

YOU are the CEO of YOUR business and you need to BELIEVE YOU ARE THE BEST for you and your staff. This MUST BE ENGRAVED!

13 - @HnTDesignMedia

A Guide to Consistent Messaging for Business

EXERCISE:

A. What are the positions and overall requirements needed for the locations of your business?

B. Do they differ between locations?

_____

_____

What are ways you will keep your staff accountable for their tasks and responsibilities?

_____

_____

How will your staff help you scale your business to the next level?

_____

_____

Your **FUNCTIONING** needs must detail the location or multiple locations of your business as well as the cost of doing business in these spaces.

Messaging for YOUR Business – Pocket Edition

The following table outlines several costs of running a business. It may not be an all-inclusive list for your business but will get you started.

NOTE: Fill in any amounts in the blank spaces. Remember, future costs are projected costs.

Cost	Amt	Additional Costs	Amt
Lights and Energy Costs		Heating and A/C Costs	
Rent / Lease Fees		Permits, Licenses, Patents, Trademarks	
Software / CRM		Conference Calling per User	
Call Center Costs		Product / Inventory Tracking	
On-Going Training Costs		Documents of Incorporation*,**	
Incident or Accident Reports		Personnel Files / Drug Testing	
Advertising Expenses		Employment Application Tracking (e.g., Indeed, HotJobs, CareerBuilder, Monsterjobs)	
Communication Logs		Tax Record Keeping	
Client Contract Files		Recurring Costs	
Startup Costs		Printing / Copying	
Postage		Domain Name /	

A Guide to Consistent Messaging for Business

Cost	Amt	Additional Costs	Amt
		Internet Fees	
Website Initiation and Maintenance		Personnel Wages / Benefits	
Office and Location Supplies		Vehicle Costs & Insurance	
Staff / Personal Training		Company Car Maintenance / Mileage	
Lawn and yard scaping maintenance or beautification		Legal Fees (e.g., rocketlawyer.com, legalzoom.com) / LLC*/DBA	
Insurance (e.g., General/product /professional liability, commercial or home-based insurance, business owner's policy)			

* - Perhaps begin with an S-Corporation – you can always convert to a C-Corporation, if needed. An LLC can be a good option for initial protection too.

** - Incorporate in the state for which your business resides.

Figure 4: Possible one-time, recurring or future costs associated with running your business

Messaging for YOUR Business – Pocket Edition

Even careful planning cannot completely eliminate risks. Having a plan can make inevitable situations easier.

Several of these can be overlooked, so it is important to think through this list and any other items so that there are little to no hidden costs.

Each type of expense or cost can add up faster than you think, so it is good to anticipate as much as possible – knowing that not every expense can or will be budgeted.

EXERCISE:

What are the one-time costs of starting your business?

_____

_____

What are the some of the recurring costs of running your business?

_____

_____

A Guide to Consistent Messaging for Business

In terms of <u>MARKETING</u>, you will see far more details as this content progresses, but marketing is how you tell people about your business. There will be ongoing marketing costs, even once people know your business exists.

For example, you will have advertising costs, paper, postage, copying, printing, supplies and decisions on what works after gaining experience. This section of your business plan should include the design work needed BEFORE you create ads or go door-to-door with your offerings.

EXERCISE:

What are your known marketing costs?

_____

_____

How will your monthly / annual budget address these costs?

_____

_____

Messaging for YOUR Business – Pocket Edition

Finally, the last area of <u>BUDGETING</u>. There will be costs and expenses that should be detailed in a statement of budget / monies that will protect you as well as the client.

Anything that causes an expense to the business should be listed in a log for each receipt. This could include legal expenses, contractual costs and more based on the type of business.

For instance, if you do social media and web design for your business, then your costs would need to include the following: software purchases, software upgrades, hardware usage, hosting services, software training, equipment rental, light bulbs and more.

NOTE: When you have a one-stop shop web business, be sure that you also have various types of contracts and documents in place, including: invoices (to get paid), model release contracts, statement of work forms and an initial questionnaire.

CHALLENGE: Oftentimes business owners underestimate not only the amount of money to be budgeted for a given period, but also the time needed for their ideas to grow into a massively-followed and supported business. As the owner, you will constantly be wearing 'many hats.'

A Guide to Consistent Messaging for Business

Do not overlook the tax benefits and liabilities regarding your budget.

RESOURCES:
https://www.hrblock.com/tax-offices/tax-prep/tax-prep-checklist-smallbusiness.html

EXERCISE:

What are the tax benefits you will have because of your business? How will you keep track of expenses? Electronic logs? Filing folders in file cabinets?

_____

_____

Now you are ready to put a name to all this back-end work. So, in the next topic, we will talk about how to name your business.

Deciding on YOUR Business Name

The first question to ask yourself is, "Who am I?"

If you do not know who YOU are as a business or business owner, then it is unlikely your clients will be able to know who YOU are as well.

Messaging for YOUR Business – Pocket Edition

That means it is important to select the parameters around your business regarding your business name. Before you even select a name, be sure that you can answer the following questions:

- *What do I offer?*
- *What do I represent?*
- *What is the scope of my business?*
- *What is my competition doing?*
- *Should I hire a naming service?*

Figure 5: Questions to ask yourself to set parameters for naming YOUR business

What do I Offer?

To answer, you must know if you will offer products, services or both.

Once you know that solidly, you must decide on the types of items offered.

Determine if you will have free products, how often the items will be upgraded and what you will label each item.

A Guide to Consistent Messaging for Business

For example, if you are going to have a multi-level coaching business, you will need to ensure that you know the packages. If you will offer individualized, one-on-one training, then your prices will inevitably be higher than if you are offering group coaching. If you are going to offer both choices, then you will need to decide the following:

- *Frequency of calls by type*
- *Type or mode of training to be offered (e.g., online training, social networking support, live coaching calls, recorded webinars, live or in-person events)*

Regardless of what you offer, you must *price* based on total value. For instance, if you are selling coffee mugs that are customized, you can sell at a higher price if there is personalization or personal appeal.

EXERCISE:

What products or services will YOUR business offer?

_____

_____

Have you vetted them in the market or with your target audience? Yes / No (Circle one response).

Messaging for YOUR Business – Pocket Edition

What do I Represent?

A name is more than just a grouping of words.

The words, with or without imagery, tell the world what you are about at a quick glance. Take for example the NIKE™ emblem. That little image is so iconic as a stand-alone graphic that no text is needed for you to think workout gear.

A name could be a single word, phrase, a name in a name or even initials of the owners. Ask a friend what he or she thinks of when they hear your naming idea, if coming up with your own name.

The name of your business may also be accompanied by a slogan that peeks a user's interest to find out more about your business.

The following are marketplace examples:

- *"I'm Lovin' it!" by McDonalds*
- *"Taste the Rainbow" by Skittles*

EXERCISE:

Brainstorm a few names based on what YOUR business represents.

_____

_____

A Guide to Consistent Messaging for Business

Name some catchy slogans for YOUR business.

_____

_____

What is the Scope of my Business?

When we hear the word *scope*, we think of boundaries for our business.

What our business will include and what our business will not include defines our work.

When YOUR business has boundaries, it sets a clear expectation in the mind of the client and lets them know what they can find, the problems you will solve and if you are the right business for their needed solution.

Remember that over time, you will have to be sure your items remain relevant. That is, items or content may need rewording, reworking or revamping to remain current.

Messaging for YOUR Business – Pocket Edition

For example, if I have a writing business and I offer to write content for a client, I need to know the style of writing, deadline, output or file type, type characteristics, topic, length, word count and general style preferred by the client.

This not only lets me know how to write the information, but also helps the client gauge whether I completed the assignment to their expectations by having clear boundaries.

CHALLENGE: Be careful when you are choosing the scope of your business. That is, it is easy for the scope to grow beyond control.

It is a good idea to start with a smaller, more manageable number of products or services and have a future product or service launch with additional items. This can be one that is celebrated once you know your selling power.

Once you celebrate with a product or services launch, be sure to revisit your offerings based on technology updates and upgrades.

A Guide to Consistent Messaging for Business

EXERCISE:

Name your first set of products or services. Write a 1-line description of each item.

_____

_____

_____

_____

What offerings will tell your clients that YOU are the right business for their needed solution?

_____

_____

How will you keep your items or offerings relevant in changing times?

_____

_____

Messaging for YOUR Business – Pocket Edition

What is my Competition doing?

The key is knowing that you have competitors AND what they do.

For instance, if you are a realtor, you will want to study and even get to know other fellow realtors in your area. It is possible that you will be in a deal with a competitor, so it is worth getting to know them face-to-face.

I always encourage business owners to go to free or economical networking events held locally. There are sites like Eventbrite™ that are great for finding such events in your area.

Additionally, you will want to know what your competitors are offering. If I return to the realtor example, here are a few questions to ask myself about my competition if I in the housing business:

- *Are they [my competitors] putting together fancy buyer packets?*
- *Are they giving free home staging?*
- *Are they offering free photography?*
- *Are they offering a free local move?*
- *Are they taking specific actions to make buyers or sellers choose them over other realtors or selling by owner?*

A Guide to Consistent Messaging for Business

Will the extra services for your clients allow you to be profitable? Think of one or more questions that your competitors cannot answer. These questions should get you thinking about how you 'stack up.'

In summary, you do not want to mimic competition, you want to use them as a guide to help YOU standout. Always be thinking about what makes your offerings new. This could mean paving the way for something that has never been done.

EXERCISE:

Name your strongest competitors by name.

Why did you name each business (e.g., qualities)?

_____

_____

Name a few ways clients can see YOU as stronger than the competition?

_____

_____

Messaging for YOUR Business – Pocket Edition

Should I Hire a Naming Service?

Naming may come easy to you, but not to others.

If you are in the latter group, do not panic, simply hire someone to take that task off your list.

Sometimes it is worth paying someone to do something so important when you lack the time to do it yourself.

There are many sites that specialize in naming businesses. This service will generally cost a fee, but some may include a logo too.

Hopefully at this point, you have selected your name, whether you named your business or you hired help. Let's talk about your logo next.

Conclusion

You have learned about the following:

- *An overview of messaging*
- *Selecting YOUR target audience*
- *The importance of having a business plan*
- *Deciding on the name of YOUR business*

You are now ready to conquer the world with your business offerings!

Other Resources

Online Course available on our website for branding your business:

https://www.handtdesignmedia.net/p/courses

Portions of this pocket book were taken from our larger branding book on Amazon at:

https://www.amazon.com/Create-Enterprise-Level-Branding-Your-Business/dp/1719475318/ref=sr_1_2?ie=UTF8&qid=1529685525&sr=8-2&keywords=beverly+reynolds+author

More courses are being added over time…

Enjoy and be sure to leave comments on our website!

www.ingramcontent.com/pod-product-compliance
Lightning Source LLC
Chambersburg PA
CBHW031600210526
45464CB00003B/1357